Original title:

Wrapped in Warmth and Winter

Author: Sophia Kingsley

ISBN HARDBACK: 978-9916-94-418-9

ISBN PAPERBACK: 978-9916-94-419-6

The Warmth Between Us

In the quiet moments, hearts align,
A gentle glow, a touch divine.
We share our dreams, our hopes, our fears,
In every smile, love's warmth appears.

Through the storms that life may send,
We'll hold each other, hand in hand.
With each heartbeat, a promise made,
The warmth between us will never fade.

Under a Quilt of Night

Stars twinkle softly in the dark,
While dreams take flight, igniting a spark.
Together we bask in silver beams,
Whispered secrets weave through our dreams.

Wrapped in shadows, our worries cease,
In the quiet night, we find our peace.
Under the quilt of the moonlit sky,
Our hearts entwine, forever nigh.

Frosted Gleams and Golden Light

Morning breaks with a frosted gleam,
The sun rises high, a golden beam.
Nature awakens in vibrant hues,
With every glance, I'm filled with muse.

Through fields aglow, we wander free,
With each soft breeze, pure harmony.
Frosted dreams dance in the bright daylight,
We'll cherish these moments, hold on tight.

Whispering Pines and Warm Hearts

In the forest deep where the stillness reigns,
Pines whisper secrets, old as the plains.
Together we stroll on this peaceful trail,
With each step we take, love will prevail.

Nature's embrace, a soothing balm,
In the chaos of life, a moment calm.
Warm hearts entwined beneath the trees,
With whispering pines, we find our peace.

Cozy Corners of December

In corners warm, the shadows play,
A golden glow at end of day.
With cups of cheer, we gather near,
And laughter dances, sweet and clear.

The frost outside, a silver lace,
Yet here, a tranquil, warm embrace.
The world grows still, the fire's light,
Transforms the dark into the bright.

Hearthside Whispers

The hearth burns low, the embers speak,
Of tales profound, of hearts so meek.
With every flicker, secrets share,
In shadows deep, in glow and glare.

We weave our dreams in whispered tones,
As winter winds dance 'round our homes.
Together here, the world can wait,
Inside this warmth, we contemplate.

Embrace of the Frost

Outside, the chill bites at the skin,
But inside, warmth is where we begin.
The frost has painted every tree,
A winter's canvas, wild and free.

We sip our tea and watch the snow,
As memories of warmth gently flow.
In cozy wraps, we find our peace,
As winter's grasp begins to cease.

Snug in the Snowfall

A blanket white, the snowflakes drift,
A world transformed, a gentle gift.
We watch from windows, eyes aglow,
As nature dances, soft and slow.

Each flake a gem, each drift a dream,
In every corner, sparkles gleam.
We bundle up in layers tight,
To face the magic of the night.

Cloaked in Softness

Whispers of the night, so still,
Wrapped in warmth, a gentle thrill.
The world outside, a distant hum,
In this cocoon, we'll never succumb.

Fluffy clouds upon the bed,
Dreams woven where love is spread.
Cloaked in softness, hearts entwined,
In this haven, sweet peace we find.

Fireside Reverie

Flames dancing in a golden glow,
Stories linger, soft and low.
With every spark, memories reign,
In this warmth, we’re free from pain.

The crackle sings a soothing tune,
Beneath the watchful eye of the moon.
Here, time slows, a cherished friend,
In fireside comfort, worries mend.

The Coziness of Hibernation

Winter's blanket calls us near,
In soft embrace, we shed all fear.
The world outside, a frosty sight,
Within these walls, we find our light.

Wrapped in layers, snug and tight,
Every moment, pure delight.
In hibernation’s gentle hold,
We weave new dreams, and tales unfold.

Sipping Cocoa Beneath the Stars

Beneath a blanket of twinkling light,
Sipping cocoa, a sweet delight.
Marshmallow clouds drift in the cup,
Each sip warms as the night lifts up.

Under the cosmos, hearts align,
Sharing secrets, yours and mine.
In this moment, time stands still,
With cocoa dreams, we dare to fill.

The Hearth's Soft Embrace

The fire crackles, warmth surrounds,
In shadows, gentle flicker found.
A cozy nook, where spirits rest,
In the hearth's embrace, we feel blessed.

With stories shared and laughter bright,
The world outside, a distant sight.
In every glow, our cares unwind,
The hearth's soft hug, so sweet and kind.

The scent of wood and embers' glow,
Here love and peace in tandem grow.
As whispers dance and brew delight,
In this soft haven, hearts take flight.

The night stretches, the stars take stage,
In this warm nook, we turn the page.
With every crackle and ember's flare,
The hearth's embrace, beyond compare.

Numbed Noses and Warm Hearts

Outside the snowflakes gently fall,
Noses red, we brave it all.
With mittens snug and scarves in place,
We chase the chill, with warmth we face.

Laughter echoes through the air,
In frosty play, we have not a care.
While cheeks are cold, our spirits sing,
Together bound, love's winter ring.

A cozy café, our refuge found,
With steaming cups, our hearts unbound.
Numbed noses fade with each sweet sip,
As warmth and joy in friendship grip.

Through snowy paths, hand in hand,
In tender moments, we understand.
Numbed noses and warm hearts unite,
In winter’s chill, we find our light.

Cocoa and Candlelight

Cocoa steaming, rich and sweet,
In candlelight, our hearts do meet.
With every sip, the soul's delight,
In cozy corners, shadows light.

The gentle glow dances on the walls,
A symphony of silence calls.
Each flicker tells a cherished tale,
In cocoa's warmth, we will not fail.

As time drifts by in soft embrace,
We linger still in this safe space.
With whispers low and laughter high,
Cocoa dreams beneath the sky.

Together bound, in sweet respite,
Cocoa and candlelight ignite.
Moments treasured, love's delight,
In such sweet warmth, we take flight.

Tucked Beneath Soft Flurries

Snowflakes swirl, a dance so light,
Tucked beneath the winter's white.
A quilt of dreams, we snuggle tight,
In soft flurries, hearts ignite.

Outside the world is hushed and still,
Inside, our love, a timeless thrill.
With blankets warm, and spirits bold,
Tucked beneath, our stories unfold.

The night is young, the stars are bright,
Each twinkling gem a guiding light.
With whispers soft, and dreams to share,
In winter's hold, there's magic rare.

Together we dream, in warm embrace,
Tucked beneath soft flurries, a sacred space.
In every breath, in every sigh,
In love's sweet warmth, we soar and fly.

Fireside Dreams

The embers glow, a soft embrace,
Whispers dance in a tranquil space.
Imagined travels on starlit streams,
Wrapped in warmth, we weave our dreams.

Crackling tales of old unfold,
Memories shared, hearts made bold.
In flickering light, we find our way,
Fireside dreams guide night to day.

A Blanket of Solace

A blanket spread on the cool, soft ground,
In the stillness, peace is found.
Night blooms gently as shadows fall,
In silence, we hear nature's call.

Stars above blink like distant friends,
On this journey, time transcends.
Wrapped in solace, hearts unite,
Finding comfort in the night.

The Chill of Nightfall

Crisp air carries a sweet refrain,
As daylight ebbs, shadows reign.
Beneath the moon's soft, silver gaze,
A hushed world lost in twilight's maze.

Whispers float on the autumn breeze,
Rustling leaves sway with such ease.
The chill awakens dreams so bright,
In the calm embrace of the night.

Cuddle Close to the Flames

The fire crackles with a lively tune,
As shadows dance beneath the moon.
Cuddle close, let worries flee,
In this warmth, we're wild and free.

Each flicker, a story to share,
In the glow, we feel no care.
With hands held tight, we brave the night,
Together we bask in the hearth's light.

Tucking Dreams Beneath the Snow

In quiet nights, the world asleep,
Whispers of dreams, buried deep.
Snowflakes dance on softly spun,
A blanket of white, where hopes are spun.

Stars peek down through frosty breath,
Each a wish, a silent quest.
Nature cradles each sweet thought,
In winter's arms, all battles fought.

Fireside Elegance

Beneath the glow of warm embrace,
The flicker of flames, a tranquil place.
Sipped tea warms the chilly air,
With tales spun softly, hearts laid bare.

Lights twinkle softly on the walls,
As laughter echoes, softly calls.
Memories weave through every heart,
In fireside elegance, never apart.

The Lure of Winter’s Charm

Silent nights, the world aglow,
Winter's charm in the gentle flow.
Footprints marked in frosty white,
Guiding hearts through the starry night.

Icicles dangle, crystal clear,
Nature's beauty, drawing near.
Each breath a cloud in the frigid air,
The lure of winter, beyond compare.

Solace in Frosty Evenings

Frosty evenings call my name,
Softly whispering, never the same.
A blanket of stars above me lies,
Cradling dreams as the cold wind sighs.

In the hush, a moment's grace,
Finding peace in the winter's embrace.
Solace found in the quiet air,
Embraced by night, free from care.

Frosted Mornings

The dawn arrives in shades of white,
Breath of winter, crisp and bright.
Silent streets, a glistening frost,
Nature's beauty, never lost.

Footprints crunch on icy ground,
Bare branches, silence all around.
Snowflakes dance, a gentle twirl,
A frosted morning, a winter swirl.

Huddled close, we sip our tea,
Warmed by hearts, in harmony.
With each breath, the chill retreats,
In frosted mornings, love repeats.

Embracing the Cold

Winter whispers, cold embrace,
Nature wraps in silvery lace.
Winds do howl, a quiet song,
In the chill, we'll grow more strong.

Together we find warmth inside,
Against the cold, we must abide.
Cozy quilts and fires bright,
Embracing all our hearts unite.

Snowflakes fall, a fleeting kiss,
In this season, we find bliss.
Hand in hand, we'll brave the night,
In the cold, we hold on tight.

Whispering Pines Under Snow

Pines stand tall, draped in white,
Whispers echo through the night.
Snowflakes settle on each bough,
Nature's magic, here and now.

Moonlight dances on the glade,
In this silence, dreams are made.
Crystals sparkle, stars align,
Whispering pines, a love divine.

Beneath the sky, we find our peace,
In the stillness, worries cease.
Nature's breath, a calming sound,
In whispering pines, joy is found.

Candlelit Hours of Reflection

Candles flicker, shadows play,
In the room, they light our way.
Thoughts take flight on gentle sighs,
In this moment, truth never lies.

Pages turn, a quiet read,
Wisdom shared, a gentle seed.
In the warmth, old stories glow,
Candlelit hours, time moves slow.

Memories dance, laughter rings,
In the light, our spirit sings.
Reflections deep, hearts connect,
Candlelit hours, we introspect.

Delights of the Dusk

Soft shadows stretch and yawn,
As daylight starts to fade.
Whispers of the night are drawn,
In twilight's sweet cascade.

Colors bleed in gentle hues,
The world begins to glow.
Stars peek out with quiet views,
As dreams start to bestow.

Crickets sing their evening song,
The breeze, it softly sighs.
In this moment, we belong,
Underneath the dusky skies.

Holding close the fading light,
As shadows start to play.
In the beauty of the night,
We find our hearts will stay.

Hearths that Warm the Soul

In the heart of winter's chill,
Firelight dances bright.
Gathered close, a cozy thrill,
Filling hearts with light.

Voices mingle, laughter flows,
Songs of warmth we share.
As the evening gently glows,
Love's a flame in the air.

Each crackle sparks a memory,
Stories told with glee.
In this space, we’re truly free,
Together, you and me.

The hearth becomes a sacred place,
Where souls can intertwine.
Wrapped in warmth, a soft embrace,
Our lives forever shine.

Frosted Windows, Warm Hearts

Frosted panes like art display,
Winter's breath and chill.
Yet within, the warmth will stay,
A love that time can't kill.

Outside, the world is crisp and white,
While heartbeats echo close.
Hand in hand, we share the night,
In warmth, we find our dose.

Every frosted sight we see,
Gleaming stars up high.
Wrapped in love and harmony,
We watch the snowflakes fly.

In this cozy, gentle space,
The winter's magic flows.
With every laugh, a sweet embrace,
Our warm hearts surely know.

Solstice Serenades

The longest night, a mystic tune,
The stars begin to gleam.
Beneath the light of silver moon,
We find our whispers dream.

Candles flicker, shadows sway,
In sacred circles near.
A symphony of night and day,
The solstice song we hear.

Voices rise in harmony,
As nature starts to sing.
The earth awakens tenderly,
Embracing everything.

In this dance of dark and light,
Hope ignites the spark.
For in the depths of winter's night,
Love will leave its mark.

Glimmers of Hope in the Chill

In the dark of the night, stars will gleam,
Whispers of warmth dance like a dream.
Frozen breath carries tales of old,
Each flicker of light, a promise bold.

A flicker of joy in the winter's chill,
Hearts beat softly, our spirits fill.
Hope's gentle glow, on this frigid night,
Guides us back home, a beacon of light.

As shadows retreat from the rising dawn,
We find our strength, our fears are gone.
With each new day, the chill will fade,
In glimmers of hope, our lives are laid.

Together we stand, hand in hand,
Braving the cold, a united band.
Through winter's grasp, we'll journey far,
Glimmers of hope, our guiding star.

Embers in the Frost

Beneath the frost, the embers glow,
A warmth that whispers, soft and low.
Winter's breath may chill the air,
But fire within ignites our care.

In the silence, stories weave,
Of battles fought and dreams to leave.
Each spark a memory, fiercely bright,
Embers dance in the quiet night.

Though shadows linger, we won't despair,
With every ember, a flame to share.
United in warmth, we’ll find our way,
Frosty nights can lead to day.

So gather near, let spirits soar,
Embers in frost, forevermore.
In the depths of winter, hearts unite,
Warming the cold with love’s pure light.

A Hearthside Embrace

Before the hearth, where warmth resides,
We gather close, where love abides.
Gentle flames flicker, stories unfold,
In this embrace, we find our gold.

Chasing away the winter's plight,
With laughter that echoes into the night.
Each moment a treasure, each breath a song,
Together we conquer, where we belong.

The crackle of wood, a soothing sound,
In this sacred space, peace is found.
A circle of hearts, forever entwined,
In a hearthside embrace, joy defined.

Through the chill that life may send,
It’s here by the fire, that hearts will mend.
A sanctuary built from love's sweet grace,
A haven of warmth, a cherished place.

Chasing Shadows of Comfort

In the twilight hour, soft and still,
Shadows beckon, a gentle thrill.
We wander through whispers of the night,
Chasing the comfort of fading light.

With each step taken, fears dissipate,
In the arms of dusk, we celebrate.
The world grows quieter, hearts align,
Finding solace in the divine.

Memories play like flickering stars,
Guiding our journey, healing our scars.
As we roam through the shadows' embrace,
We find our peace in this sacred space.

So let us chase what brings us near,
In the shadows, we conquer fear.
For comfort lies in the paths we tread,
In the warmth of connection, we are led.

The Lullaby of Winter Nights

Snowflakes whisper in the breeze,
Gentle dreams beneath the trees.
Stars are dancing in the sky,
Softly, night begins to sigh.

Candles flicker, shadows play,
Hopes abound at end of day.
Warmth wraps round like a soft shawl,
In winter's cradle, we hear its call.

Blankets pile on cozy beds,
Silent wishes, softly said.
A lullaby of peace and rest,
In winter's arms, we feel the best.

Serenity Beneath the Icicles

Icicles hanging, shimmering bright,
Nature's jewels in moonlight.
Crisp air whispers sweet allure,
In stillness found, we feel secure.

Trees stand guard, their branches bare,
A secret world, we'll gently share.
Footprints trace where few have tread,
Among the snow, where dreams are shed.

With every breath, serenity flows,
As winter's magic gently glows.
In the silence, hearts unite,
Underneath the calm, soft light.

Warmth in a Glass

Steam arises from the brew,
In a cup of comfort, warm and true.
Spices dance with cozy cheer,
In every sip, love draws near.

Fall leaves swirl against the glass,
Reminders of the seasons past.
With every taste, we find our peace,
As worries fade and troubles cease.

A gathering of friends and smiles,
In laughter shared, we find our miles.
Warmth in a glass, a gentle way,
To toast the bonds that light our day.

Homebound Comfort

The hearth aglow, the fire's light,
Home's embrace feels just so right.
Familiar scents of warmth and care,
In every corner, memories share.

A kettle sings upon the stove,
Wrapped in blankets, loved, and roved.
Chasing shadows, softly we laugh,
In our haven, we take a path.

Windows fogged from breath and sighs,
Outside the world, a snowy guise.
But inside, joy is here to stay,
Homebound comfort lights our way.

The Chill’s Tender Touch

In the morning mist, so cool and bright,
Frosty tendrils kiss the dawn's first light.
Whispers of winter dance through the trees,
A gentle reminder, as soft as a breeze.

Each breath a cloud, a fleeting sigh,
Nature sleeps under a pale, gray sky.
The world stands still, in serene embrace,
As the chill's touch brings a tranquil grace.

Snowflakes and Radiant Hearts

Falling softly, the snowflakes twirl,
Each one unique, like a precious pearl.
They blanket the earth, so pure and white,
A canvas of dreams, so dazzling bright.

Hearts flutter like wings with every flake,
In the magic of winter, love’s promise awakes.
Together we dance, through the shimmering night,
Two souls in the silence, wrapped up so tight.

Beneath Wooly Layers

Cocooned in warmth, beneath layers we hide,
The world outside waits, a chilled, frosty tide.
With cocoa in hand, laughter fills the air,
As stories unfold, without a single care.

Beneath wooly layers, we find our retreat,
Wrapped in comfort, where hearts skip a beat.
The season of stillness, we cherish and hold,
In the warmth of our love, we brave the cold.

Pine-Scented Serenity

In forests deep, where tall pines sway,
A fragrance of peace, in nature's array.
Amidst the branches, time moves slow,
In each gentle whisper, life's secrets flow.

The soft crunch of needles, beneath our feet,
A harmony found, where the earth and sky meet.
Pine-scented serenity, a soothing balm,
In this tranquil haven, our spirits stay calm.

Frosty Paths to Tranquility

Footsteps crunch on sparkling white,
Whispers of peace in the cool night.
Each breath clouds in the chilly air,
Nature's embrace, a gentle care.

Wander through the silent trees,
Branches hold crystal memories.
Softly glows the moon above,
Guiding us with winter's love.

Every path holds tales untold,
In frost and silence, we behold.
A world wrapped in soft despair,
Breath of winter, fresh and rare.

Through the calm, we find our way,
Frosty paths where shadows play.
In tranquility, hearts revive,
In the cold, we come alive.

Laughter On Ice

Children twirl on gleaming sheets,
Echoes of joy with every feat.
Laughter dances on frozen ground,
Pure delight in every sound.

Snowflakes swirl in dizzying flight,
Chasing dreams in the winter light.
Slides and spins, the world feels right,
Hearts are warm on this cold night.

Footfalls trace a wondrous art,
Friendships forged, a warming heart.
Every slip, a chuckle shared,
Moments made, everyone cared.

Beneath the starry, frosty sky,
Joyful voices soar and fly.
In every smile, pure delight,
Life is good, laughter takes flight.

The Comfort of Flurries

Softly falling, white as lace,
Flurries dance, a gentle grace.
Cocooned in warmth, we watch and sigh,
As winter's magic passes by.

Each flake tells a story clear,
Whispers of comfort, drawing near.
Fires crackle, glowing bright,
Inside our hearts, pure delight.

Wrapped in shawls, we share our dreams,
Hot cocoa flows in swirling streams.
In the stillness, peace does bloom,
While flurries swirl around the room.

As night descends and shadows creep,
Winter whispers us to sleep.
In dreams of snow, our spirits soar,
A world of wonder, we adore.

Seasons of Snug Refuge

When winter winds begin to blow,
The world turns white, a peaceful glow.
In cozy nooks, we find our place,
Wrapped in warmth, a sweet embrace.

Fires crackle, stories shared,
In simple joys, we are prepared.
Throw another log, let time pause,
Nature's beauty leaves us in awe.

With frosty breath and twinkling lights,
We cozy in through winter nights.
Blankets pulled and candles gleam,
Together we weave our dreams.

The seasons change but love remains,
In snug refuge, joy sustains.
Through storms outside, our hearts are free,
In warmth, we build our harmony.

Icicle-Sculpted Dreams

Icicles hang like crystal tears,
Reflecting dreams of cold white years.
Each drip a whisper, soft and clear,
In winter's lap, we shed our fears.

Frozen landscapes stretch afar,
Beneath a sky, a silver star.
In silence deep, our hearts do gleam,
Awake within this icy dream.

Shimmering light on blanket white,
Time stands still, a frozen flight.
We wander through this frigid scheme,
In the world of icicle dreams.

Lost in wonder, hand in hand,
Together here, we make our stand.
With every breath, the cold air seams,
Awakening our fairy dreams.

The Snugness of Silence

In the hush of evening's glow,
Blankets thick, the fire's low.
Snowflakes dance outside the light,
Wrapping us in cozy night.

The world retreats, just you and I,
Underneath the starlit sky.
Time drips slowly, moments cease,
In this snugness, we find peace.

Voices soften, laughter fades,
As winter's charm in silence wades.
Together here, within this space,
The warmth of love, our soft embrace.

In stories shared and whispers sweet,
Our hearts align, and pulses meet.
With every heartbeat, love's design,
The snugness of our silence shines.

Gentle Embraces of the Frost

Frostkisses brush against the pane,
Transforming breath to soft white rain.
In gentle holds, the world feels new,
Wrapped in winter's tender cue.

Each step we take on crunching snow,
Leaves behind a tale in tow.
With every chill, the air ignites,
Creating magic in wintry nights.

Soft whispers weave through nippy air,
A loving touch, so light and rare.
In shadows cast by pale moon's glow,
Frosted dreams begin to flow.

Gentle embraces, heartfelt sighs,
Underneath these painted skies.
In winter's arms, we twirl and spin,
Together lost, where love begins.

A Winter's Tapestry

Threads of white, the world's attire,
A quilt of cold, in icy fire.
Nature's brush depicts the scene,
A winter's tale, serene and keen.

Pine trees stand in stoic grace,
Adorned with snow, a silent place.
Each flake weaves through the frosty air,
In this tapestry, we share.

Scattered whispers weave delight,
In painted strokes of black and white.
Together here, stitched with care,
A winter's dream, we both ensnare.

Underneath the quiet skies,
We find our hearts where stillness lies.
In laughter shared, we gently sway,
A masterpiece of winter's day.

Enchanted by the Chill

A whispering breeze cuts through the still,
Glistening snowflakes dance, a wink, a thrill.
Trees stand tall, their branches bare,
Nature wrapped in winter's care.

The softest hush blankets the night,
Dreams drift softly in pale moonlight.
Every corner sparkles, pure and white,
Enchantment lives in the silent flight.

Frosty air, a crisp embrace,
Time slows down, we find our place.
In this realm of quiet grace,
Life pauses, lost in winter's space.

Hearts entwined in whispers low,
Warmth found beneath the cold snow.
Together we wander, hand in hand,
In this enchanted, frosted land.

The Embrace of Shadows

In twilight's hold, shadows creep,
Whispering secrets, promises deep.
The darkness drapes with tender care,
A soft embrace, a silent prayer.

The moon becomes a guiding light,
As stars awake to grace the night.
In the quiet, fears take flight,
The embrace of shadows feels just right.

Figures dance under the dome,
Every heartbeat calls them home.
In the stillness, we find our song,
The shadows cradle where we belong.

Glimmers weave through the black,
With each heartbeat, we won't look back.
In the presence of the soft unknown,
We discover worlds, together grown.

Winter’s Heartfelt Hug

Snowflakes drift like gentle sighs,
Filling the world with frosty ties.
A heartfelt hug from winter's breath,
A soothing warmth beyond mere death.

Each flake unique, a tale to tell,
In the silence, we know it well.
Embraced in layers, thick and lush,
Winter's magic brings a soothing hush.

Inside we gather, stories to share,
Laughter echoes, fills the air.
Outside, the world wears icy crowns,
While warmth continues to break down frowns.

Together we stand, together we stay,
In winter's heart while skies turn grey.
A love that glows in the chill's tight grip,
With every hug, our spirits lift.

The Light in Winter's Grasp

In winter's grasp, the light does glow,
Soft and gentle, a warming flow.
Kissed by sunlight, the icicles gleam,
A dance of warmth, like a waking dream.

The world sparkles, a diamond show,
Beneath the cover of purest snow.
Hope rises bright against the cold,
In winter's heart, stories unfold.

As days stretch long, shadows grow thin,
Life awakens, the light pours in.
With every dawn, a chance to start,
Guided by the glow that fills the heart.

So let us cherish this fleeting show,
Of light in winter, with love we grow.
In every moment, find the spark,
Illuminating paths in the world so dark.

The Uniform of Cold

The frost lays a blanket so white,
Covering fields in shimmering light.
Branches sparkle like diamonds bright,
In the stillness, the world feels right.

Breathe in the air, sharp and clear,
A chilling whisper, drawing near.
Nature wears its quiet attire,
As snowflakes dance, the world conspire.

Footsteps crunch on frozen ground,
Echoes of silence all around.
Winter's breath, a soft embrace,
In this frozen, sacred space.

The moon hangs low, a lantern's glow,
Casting shadows, a silver show.
The night wraps all in its gentle hold,
Nature's muse, in uniform of cold.

Whispered Secrets in the Dark

In the shadows where whispers dwell,
Softened tones of secrets tell.
Moonlight weaves through the trees,
Carrying secrets on the breeze.

Stars flicker like distant dreams,
Bathed in silvery, quiet beams.
All around, the night bestows,
Mysteries where the darkness grows.

Eyes closed tight, the heart can hear,
Secrets shared without a fear.
Voices hushed in the cool, still air,
Entwined souls in a tranquil prayer.

As night deepens, shadows blend,
A sanctuary where tales extend.
Each word a thread, delicately spun,
In the tapestry of the dark, they run.

Heartbeats Among the Frost

In the hush of a winter's night,
Heartbeats echo, pure and bright.
Among the frost, a rhythm plays,
In soft whispers, love displays.

Golden glows from windows beam,
Fires crackle, a steady stream.
Hands entwined, a gentle hold,
Warmth found in a world so cold.

Against the chill, bodies sway,
Creating warmth in a frosty ballet.
Laughter dances on the air,
Love's sweet promise, always there.

In the silence, hearts align,
Drawing warmth from love divine.
Among the frost, two souls are lost,
Beating on, whatever the cost.

Twilight's Gentle Caress

As the sun dips below the hill,
Twilight unfurls, a tranquil thrill.
Colors bleed into the night,
Whispers thread the fading light.

Crickets strum their evening song,
Nature's voice, both soft and strong.
Shadows stretch as day retreats,
Swaying gently in twilight's beats.

Stars awaken, one by one,
Embers of the day's bright sun.
In this moment, time feels slow,
In twilight's arms, we find our glow.

Embrace the dusk, let worries part,
In the stillness, find your heart.
With every breath, a calming press,
Wrapped in twilight's gentle caress.

The Poetry of Ice Crystals

A shimmer in the morning light,
Each crystal spins, pure and bright.
Fragile beauty on window panes,
Whispers of winter in soft refrains.

Nature's art in a frozen form,
A silent spell that's calm and warm.
Delicate lace, a fleeting show,
Crafted by winds that gently blow.

Time stands still in its cold embrace,
Every twinkle a joyous trace.
Life slows down, the world in white,
A canvas gleaming, pure delight.

As sunlight fades, the twilight glows,
Ice crystals dance, a gentle pose.
In the night, they glow and gleam,
A winter's magic, a shimmering dream.

Chestnuts and Old Records

In the corner, chestnuts lie,
Hushed whispers of days gone by.
Old records spin with a crackling tune,
Nostalgic notes beneath the moon.

The warmth of fire, the scent of roast,
Memories cherished, a comforting host.
Each needle drop brings laughter near,
Echoes of voices we hold dear.

Frayed edges tell tales, softly spun,
Stories of life and joy, each one.
Fingers trace grooves like old friends,
A melody linger, never ends.

Amidst the crackles, the chestnuts pop,
In a world of music, we never stop.
We gather close, share stories and cheer,
In the warmth of the night, all we hold dear.

The Dance of Shadows in Winter

Beneath the trees, shadows stretch long,
Winter's breath sings a silent song.
Figures shift in the pale moonlight,
A ghostly waltz that feels so bright.

Snowflakes twirl, in the stillness they play,
Casting dreams that softly sway.
A dance of shadows, a waltz of frost,
In this quiet realm, nothing is lost.

Branches cradle the stars above,
Whispers of winter, echoes of love.
In every step, a story unfolds,
Of dark and light, and secrets told.

As moments pass in this frozen land,
The shadows dance, both soft and grand.
A fleeting glimpse of what might be,
In winter's embrace, we wander free.

Winter's Gentle Caress

A breath of stillness in the air,
Winter wraps us with tender care.
Blankets of white on quiet streets,
Nature’s pause where serenity meets.

Gentle whispers of frosty breath,
Life slows down in the calm of death.
Birds tucked in, as silence reigns,
Soft echoes linger, a sweet refrain.

Icicles hang like crystal spears,
Witnesses to our quiet fears.
Yet in this chill, warmth can ignite,
Hearts joined together, burning bright.

Winter's embrace, a time to heal,
In its stillness, we learn to feel.
With every flake that graces the ground,
Love's gentle touch in silence found.

Rhythms of Winter's Embrace

The snowflakes dance in twilight's hush,
A quiet world in nature's brush.
Fires crackle, warming hearts,
As winter's song, the stillness starts.

Crisp air whispers secrets old,
In every flake, a tale is told.
Footsteps crunch on paths of white,
Witness to the gentle night.

Stars peek down through branches bare,
Their twinkling eyes, a watchful stare.
Underneath the moon's soft glow,
The rhythms of winter flow.

Embraced by calm, the world retreats,
In chilling warmth, our spirit meets.
In every shadow, stories thread,
As winter whispers: we are fed.

Nighttime Adventures in a Cozy Nook

In a cozy nook, the lanterns sway,
Casting dreams in shades of gray.
Books piled high with tales untold,
Whispers of adventures bold.

Outside, the stars in silent flight,
Inside, the world feels soft and bright.
A cup of tea, warm in hand,
As stories drift, both grand and planned.

Each turn of page ignites the night,
Lost in legends, hearts take flight.
With every word, new worlds appear,
In this corner, peace draws near.

Time flows slow, like rivers wide,
In this haven, dreams collide.
Night unfolds with gentle grace,
Adventures linger in this place.

The Stillness of Scented Pine

In forests deep, where echoes sigh,
The scented pine reaches to the sky.
Whispers carried on the breeze,
Nature's calm, a soul to ease.

Soft moss carpets the weary ground,
In this stillness, peace is found.
Branches sway, a gentle dance,
Inviting all to share a glance.

Sunlight filters through the green,
Casting shadows, a tranquil scene.
The world outside fades far away,
In scented pine, we choose to stay.

With every breath, the heart aligns,
In this embrace of ancient pines.
A tranquil heart, a quiet mind,
In nature's arms, serenity we find.

Turning Pages in the Glow

In the evening glow, a tale unfolds,
With every page, new dreams take hold.
The crackling fire paints the room,
As stories lift the heart from gloom.

Fingers trace the words so light,
In soft illumination, worlds ignite.
With every chapter, journeys start,
A dance of words to warm the heart.

Outside, the night has wrapped its cloak,
Inside, laughter and dreams provoke.
With each new line, we drift away,
To places where our spirits play.

Turning pages in soft embrace,
Lost in time, we find our place.
In the glow, our souls entwine,
As stories weave, the stars align.

Wrapped in Nature's Embrace

Leaves rustle softly in the breeze,
Whispers of the earth's sweet charms.
Sunlight filters through the trees,
Nature wraps us in her arms.

Birdsong dances in the air,
Flowers bloom in vibrant hues.
Every moment, a gentle prayer,
In the wild, our spirit renews.

Mountains stand with ancient pride,
Rivers flow with tales untold.
In this beauty, we confide,
Nature's warmth, a heart of gold.

Here we breathe, here we belong,
Crickets chirp as night descends.
In nature's chorus, we are strong,
In her embrace, our soul transcends.

Echoes of Winter

Cold winds whisper through the trees,
Blanketing the world in white.
Footsteps crunch as time flees,
Under dim and fading light.

Frosty breath in the chilly air,
Silent nights with stars aglow.
Memories linger everywhere,
In the stillness, we feel the snow.

Icicles hang like crystal tears,
Nature's art, a fleeting show.
Each moment holds a thousand years,
In winter's hush, our spirits grow.

As the earth sleeps under its quilt,
Hopes are whispered on the breeze.
In this magic, we are built,
Embraced by winter's gentle freeze.

A Symphony of Snow and Solitude

Snowflakes twirl in graceful flight,
A quiet world wrapped up in grace.
Silence deepens with the night,
In solitude, we find our place.

Footprints lead to distant dreams,
Crystals glisten, softly gleam.
The moon above, a silver beam,
In winter's chill, all is as it seems.

Whispers of the falling snow,
Nature's symphony unfolds.
A calm warmth begins to grow,
In this stillness, life beholds.

Hope is woven through the frost,
In every flake, a story spun.
In this solitude, nothing's lost,
Just a moment—we are one.

The Warmth of Old Stories

By the fire, embers glow bright,
Echoes of laughter fill the air.
Tales of old bring pure delight,
As memories linger everywhere.

In the shadows, wisdom sits,
Passed from hearts to eager minds.
Every word, a treasure fits,
Binding souls, as time unwinds.

The warmth of voices, soft and low,
Wraps around like a cherished quilt.
Each tale shared ignites the glow,
In our hearts, the flame is built.

As stars shine bright in the vast night,
Our stories dance across the sky.
In every moment, pure delight,
The warmth of old stories never die.

Cradled by the Season

In the arms of autumn's glow,
Leaves like whispers start to flow.
Golden hues paint the trees,
A gentle chill rides the breeze.

Frosted mornings greet the day,
Sunlight dances, skies turn gray.
Nature's quilt wraps the land,
Chasing shadows, soft and grand.

Winter's breath speaks soft and low,
Echoes of a time to snow.
Every branch adorned with white,
Cradled dreams by starry night.

Springtime blooms with colors bright,
Awakening from winter's night.
Life returns with vibrant grace,
Cradled in nature's warm embrace.

Blankets of Whispered Dreams

Underneath the starry veil,
Whispers weave a gentle tale.
Cubed in shadows, soft and deep,
Wrapped in dreams, we drift to sleep.

Moonlight laces through the trees,
Breath of night carried by the breeze.
Every sigh and every sound,
Blankets of love wrap us around.

In the stillness, hearts take flight,
Floating softly through the night.
The world outside begins to fade,
In whispered dreams, our hopes are laid.

Morning brings a soft embrace,
Sunrise paints a glowing trace.
But in our hearts, we hold so near,
Blankets of dreams forever clear.

Candlelight and Snowflakes

Flickering flames in the quiet dark,
Candlelight creates a spark.
Snowflakes dance through the chilly air,
Whispers of winter, soft and rare.

Each flake tells a unique story,
Twinkling in a world of glory.
With every glow and every sigh,
Time slows down as dreams pass by.

Winter evenings wrapped in peace,
Moments caught that never cease.
Candlelight casts a tender glow,
While snowflakes flutter soft and slow.

In this stillness, love ignites,
Hearts come alive on cozy nights.
Together by the fire's warm light,
Candlelight and snowflakes unite.

Enveloping Silence of Snowfall

A quiet world beneath the snow,
Softly resting, time moves slow.
Whispers of winter linger near,
Enveloping all in silvery cheer.

Each flake a hush, a gentle sigh,
Filling the space where dreams can fly.
Nature holds its breath in grace,
As snowflakes cover all in lace.

Footsteps muffled, sound does fade,
A tapestry of peace is laid.
In the heart of winter's chill,
Silence speaks, a tranquil thrill.

Moments stretch, the world stands still,
Enveloping silence, a soothing thrill.
In this magic, we find our way,
Snowfall's embrace, a soft ballet.

Silent Starlit Chill

Beneath the quiet night sky,
Stars shimmer and softly sigh.
A gentle breeze whispers low,
In the heart of winter's glow.

Snowflakes dance through the air,
Floating dreams without a care.
Each one a secret untold,
In their silence, a world unfolds.

The moon watches, calm and bright,
Casting shadows, soft and light.
Footprints trace along the way,
In the hush, where dreams can play.

Winter's breath, a frosty kiss,
In the stillness, a moment's bliss.
Wrapped in layers, warm and tight,
We embrace the starry night.

The Glow of Short Days

As daylight slips into the night,
A warm glow, a soft delight.
Golden hues paint the sky,
In fleeting moments, time slips by.

Fires crackle, embers glow,
Winter's night, a gentle show.
Hot cocoa warms chilly hands,
We gather close where love expands.

The scent of pine fills the room,
As the world outside finds gloom.
Together we share stories told,
In laughter, our hearts unfold.

Short days pale into dark,
Yet in our hearts, there’s a spark.
In the quiet, warmth remains,
A glow of love, despite the rains.

Frost-Kissed Memories

Frosted edges on the glass,
Whispers of the winters past.
Memories wrapped tight with cheer,
In our minds, they linger near.

Laughter echoes through the years,
In every joy, in every tear.
Footprints left in the snow,
Tales of warmth that ever glow.

The stories held in frozen air,
Recalling moments, sweet and rare.
Time may fade, but not the heart,
In each frost, a work of art.

Gathered 'round as shadows blend,
In this chill, our spirits mend.
Together, we weave a dream,
Frost-kissed memories, like a gleam.

Layers of Laughter and Snow

In the hush of falling snow,
Laughter dances, warm and slow.
Children play, their voices rise,
Joy and magic fill the skies.

Building snowmen, cheeks aglow,
Each layer wrapped in laughter's flow.
Warmth beneath the cold's embrace,
In every smile, a cherished space.

Footsteps crunch on icy trails,
As winter tells its frosty tales.
Sleds race down the hills so steep,
In the chill, our spirits leap.

Layers thick with love and cheer,
In the heart, we hold it dear.
Winter's wonder, bright and true,
In layers of laughter, me and you.

The Dance of Lights and Shadows

In twilight's glow, the shadows play,
Flickering forms drift softly away.
A whispered breeze moves through the trees,
As day retreats on gentle knees.

Stars ignite the velvet sky,
While moonlight glistens, soft and shy.
The dance unfolds, a silent waltz,
In the world where darkness exalts.

Echoes collide where silence breathes,
In the embrace of autumn leaves.
Light and shadow, hand in hand,
Create a portrait, grand and grand.

In every crack and crevice deep,
The secrets of the night we keep.
A symphony of dim and bright,
In the magic of the night.

Serenity in the Cold

The world is draped in tranquil white,
As snowflakes fall, a silent rite.
Each breath released, a cloud of mist,
In winter's grasp, the time is kissed.

Bare branches stretch, embracing fate,
Each moment lingers, still and great.
The chill around, a gentle hug,
In this serenity, I am snug.

Footsteps crunch on frozen ground,
A symphony of peace surrounds.
In stillness lives a quiet song,
Where hearts can mend and spirits long.

Wrapped in layers, warm and dear,
I find my solace, crystal clear.
In the cold, my thoughts take flight,
Finding warmth in the soft light.

An Oven’s Lullaby

The oven hums a gentle tune,
As warmth envelops afternoon.
With every rise, a promise swells,
In fragrant realms, where magic dwells.

Golden crust and tender core,
With flavors rich, we all adore.
A dance of yeast and flour's grace,
In kitchen's heart, our happy place.

Beneath the heat, the beauty grows,
A simple art that love bestows.
As timers chime, anticipation,
In this embrace, sweet celebration.

From oven's glow, to table's light,
Connections formed, a pure delight.
In every loaf, a story shared,
An oven's lullaby, declared.

Cozy Corners of Reflection

In quiet nooks where shadows blend,
A cup of tea becomes a friend.
With whispered thoughts, the silence speaks,
In cozy corners, calmness peaks.

The world outside, a distant hum,
While here, my thoughts softly come.
Pages turn in gentle light,
As dreams unfold, a wondrous flight.

Through windowpanes, the rain cascades,
A soothing sound that never fades.
I find my peace in this embrace,
Each moment savored, time can't chase.

In cozy corners, I reside,
With every heartbeat, love as guide.
Reflections dance, in shadows cast,
In simple joy, the heart beats fast.

Interludes in the Icicles

Crystal shards in sunlight play,
Hanging still while moments sway.
Whispers of a winter's song,
Nature's breath, both soft and strong.

Fractured light, a dance so bright,
Silent guardians of the night.
Every droplet tells a tale,
Of frosty paths and whispers pale.

Echoes of the past unfold,
Tales of ice and dreams untold.
In the chill, a warmth will rise,
As the world beneath it sighs.

Through the frost, a vision wide,
Finding joy where shadows glide.
Interludes of glistening white,
Paint the canvas, pure delight.

A Warm Glow Amid the Chill

Candle flames in twilight glow,
Casting shadows, soft and slow.
Hear the crackle, feel the heat,
A haven found, where hearts can meet.

Snowflakes dance on winter's breath,
Whispers sweet, defying death.
In this space, love threads its way,
Through the night, inviting play.

Blankets wrapped, a cozy dome,
In this warmth, we find our home.
Hand in hand, we brave the cold,
Stories shared and secrets told.

With each sip of spiced delight,
We build a world to chase the night.
A warm glow, through all the chill,
Hearts awake, and spirits thrill.

Dreams of Pine and Flickering Flame

In a forest, shadows loom,
Pine trees sway, as night consumes.
Flickering flames in distance spark,
Illuminating paths through dark.

Whispers of the gentle breeze,
Carrying tales among the trees.
Every crackle, every sigh,
Brings enchantment from the sky.

Dreams arise from embers' glow,
Stories waiting, deep below.
In that moment, time stands still,
Capturing hearts with every thrill.

Let the night be filled with grace,
In this haven, our sacred space.
Together here, by fire's frame,
We weave our dreams, a timeless game.

Heartfelt Echoes of Solstice

In the longest light of day,
Whispers dance in golden rays,
Promises of change ascend,
Nature's song, a faithful friend.

Shadows stretch as warmth will fade,
Each moment, memories made,
Laughter mingles with the breeze,
Time stands still beneath the trees.

In twilight's glow, we find our place,
Holding hands, a soft embrace,
Stars awaken, night takes hold,
Heartfelt stories, yet untold.

Solstice gifts a chance to see,
The beauty in just you and me,
With every echo from the past,
We cherish moments, love held fast.

Muffled Laughter in the Chill

Snowflakes fall with gentle grace,
Covering the world, a white embrace,
Children's laughter fills the air,
In the cold, there’s warmth to share.

Jack Frost paints the windowpane,
Each breath visible, like soft rain,
Footprints mark a playful race,
Muffled joy in winter's space.

Hot cocoa warms our frozen hands,
As firelight flickers, joy expands,
Stories shared, hearts open wide,
In the chill, our love won't hide.

Underneath the starlit skies,
Together, we find joy that lies,
In the quiet, laughter flows,
Muffled echoes, winter's prose.

A Tapestry of Frosted Breath

Morning whispers in shades of white,
Frosted breath in soft daylight,
Nature dons a sparkling gown,
As silence wraps the sleepy town.

Branches glisten, diamonds freeze,
In stillness, hearts find ease,
Each moment stitched with care,
A tapestry of winter rare.

Footsteps crunch on snowy ground,
In this quiet, peace is found,
The world awakes in muted tones,
As every breath, a gentle moan.

In the chill, warmth still exists,
A tapestry of love subsists,
With every sigh, stories weave,
In frosted breath, we believe.

Gentle Mornings Wrapped in Silk

Dawn breaks softly, colors blend,
A canvas where our dreams transcend,
Sunlight spills like honey sweet,
In a world, where stillness greets.

Silk embrace of growing light,
Cocooned in warmth, everything feels right,
Birds arise with melodies bright,
Morning whispers, pure delight.

Coffee brews, the scent divine,
As laughter mingles, yours and mine,
Gentle moments, slowly unfurl,
In the quiet, our hearts swirl.

Wrapped in silk and soft embrace,
Time drifts on at its own pace,
Each day a gift, a treasure rare,
In gentle mornings, love's sweet air.

Sheltered from the Storm

In the heart of the night, so deep,
The winds howl and the shadows creep.
But behind these sturdy walls, I'm safe,
In the glow of the fire, my heart finds grace.

Raindrops tap on the windowpane,
Whispers of nature, a soft refrain.
Wrapped in a blanket, my worries cease,
All is calm here, and my soul finds peace.

Outside, the world may twist and bend,
But inside, I know this warmth won't end.
Each flicker of light, a gentle kiss,
Moments like these, I can't help but miss.

So I stay sheltered, with thoughts so warm,
Safe and sound, away from the storm.
With dreams that dance like the embers bright,
I cherish this solace on this lonely night.

Flickering Flames and Falling Snow

Fires crackle, bright and bold,
While snowflakes dance in a hush of gold.
Each ember glows, a story told,
In winter's chill, warmth unfolds.

Outside, the world is a silver dome,
But here by the flames, we feel at home.
With cups of cheer, we laugh and play,
Creating memories that won't fade away.

The snow may blanket the earth so wide,
But here in our hearts, joy will abide.
As flames flicker soft, our worries cease,
In this magical moment, we find our peace.

So let the snow fall, let the winds blow,
Here by the fire, we'll let our hearts grow.
In the dance of the night, in the warmth we find,
Flickering flames and falling snow intertwined.

The Essence of Hot Chocolate

In a cup of warmth, joy brewed in delight,
Rich chocolate swirls on a cold winter's night.
With marshmallows melting, a soft, creamy dream,
Each sip is a hug, like a soft, warming beam.

Spices whisper secrets, a dash of sweet thrill,
As I cradle my cup, the world feels still.
In every rich drop, memories reside,
Of laughter and love, all time cannot hide.

Steam rises softly, wrapping me tight,
In moments like these, everything feels right.
A cozy embrace from the inside out,
In the essence of cocoa, there's never a doubt.

So here's to each mug, filled to the brim,
To the warmth that it brings when the days feel dim.
In the heart of winter, a simple delight,
Hot chocolate's essence shines so bright.

Sledding Into Warmth

Down the hill, with laughter loud,
On a sled, we race like a joyful crowd.
The crisp air bites, but spirits soar,
With each wild ride, we crave more and more.

Snowflakes tumble, a soft white veil,
As we glide through winter, our hearts set sail.
Through trees we weave, the world a blur,
In this fleeting moment, all our cares concur.

But now it’s time, as shadows grow,
To seek out warmth from the icy show.
Hot cocoa waits as we walk through the door,
Embracing the fire, the chill we ignore.

So here's to the thrill and the joy unsung,
To sledding adventures and songs still sung.
In every descent, love shares its norm,
We find our solace, sledding into warmth.